Praise for TYPE 2 DIA
FOR REAL

"This is an easy to read, high, practical book.
The author has tackled a big issue and
presented an easy-to-follow eating plan
with straightforward recipes
suitable for any family."

"Very helpful and got the diet started straightaway
with minimum fuss."

"Very easy to follow recipes that
have clearly been well researched."

"Excellent tips and recipes."

"Nice, easy and straightforward meals."

"Excellent help to diabetics."

"Very informative."

"Easy to follow recipes with clear instructions."

"Great practical tips and information."

"This book is great for people who have been
diagnosed with type 2 diabetes and
have no idea what to do."

"The recipes are suitable for the whole family."

Susan Hegedus is an author and freelance writer.
She grew up in the East End of London
and now lives in Billericay, Essex.

Susan has a BA(Hons) English degree and
her book *The Hidden Green Man in Essex*
was published in 2011.

She writes for various magazines and
enjoys exploring medieval churches,
playing the flute and eating.

Find out more about Susan:
www.susanhegedus.com

Susan Hegedus

Type 2 Diabetes Cookbook

for

Real Men

A 7-Day Eating Plan with Recipes

Luscious Books

Published by Luscious Books Ltd 2016
Morwellham, Down Park Drive, Tavistock, PL19 9AH, Great Britain

ISBN 978-1-910929-05-6

www.lusciousbooks.co.uk

Contents

Disclaimer

The information provided in this book is not a substitute for professional medical care, advice or guidance from a doctor or other suitably qualified healthcare professional. It cannot be warranted that any information included in this book will meet your particular health or medical requirements.

It is very important that you seek medical advice from a doctor or other suitably qualified healthcare professional if you have any concerns or questions about your health and diet.

The author of this book is not a medical doctor. This book merely contains information and recipes that she has found useful.

Introduction

So you have type 2 diabetes? Perhaps you've been recently diagnosed? Don't panic! You are not going to be condemned to a lifetime of bland chicken salads. Help is at hand. You can still enjoy great food and the odd treat – really!

I shall never forget the day my husband Anthony came home from the doctor's and announced that he was a diabetic. We were both in shock. This medical label had suddenly attached itself to him. I knew he would have to change his diet. But where were we supposed to begin? This man loved bacon sandwiches and pot noodles! How was he going to break the habits of a lifetime?

I can't pretend our first few weeks were easy. We were new to the world of diabetes, and he kicked against the idea of special meals. So I began to prepare diabetic-friendly meals for the whole family rather than cooking separately.

My aim was to produce healthy meals which didn't compromise on taste. I knew whole foods were much better than processed foods and that was my starting point. I certainly didn't want to be diving for the glycemic index manual every time I cooked something. I realized diabetic eating was about moderation – not depriving yourself.

Also, as my husband was not keen on 'rabbit food', I tailored the meals so they did not include salads or too many fancy vegetables. Only 'food for real men' was on the menu. He has been happy with my approach, and as they say, the proof of the pudding is in the eating: my husband's glycated hemoglobin level has dropped substantially. We have never looked back!

How to use this book?

I have devised a 7-day eating plan suitable for 'real men' who'd rather avoid salads and instead eat honest hearty food. The recipes are among my family's favorites. They are all easy to make and your time is spent eating rather than cooking. What's even more wonderful: you can have a dessert each day if you wish!

If you're looking for meal and snack ideas, follow the easy 7-day plan and avoid the potentially complicated task of having to work out what to eat. The plan offers suggestions for breakfast, lunch, snacks and dinner (including that all important dessert!)

If you prefer to plan your meals yourself and you're just looking for some new diabetic-friendly recipes, go straight to the recipe section. There you can find delicious meals for every day of the week.

I've included a chapter on ingredients and healthy eating in this book. It offers some tips about eating and cooking for diabetics. It's not a comprehensive guide though, so if you'd like to find out more, there's a lot of information available online. I would also recommend you discuss your particular needs with your physician, dietician or other qualified medical professional.

Tips about ingredients and healthy eating

Beverages

Water

Water is possibly the best beverage to drink. You don't necessarily have to buy bottled water as in most places clear cold water from the tap is acceptable.

If you get into the habit of drinking more water, you may not feel so hungry when your next snack or meal is due. This can help with weight loss. Furthermore, drinking plenty of water may help your body to absorb the nutrients in food and remove toxins from your body. It's a cheap way of improving your general wellbeing.

Tea and coffee

Tea and coffee contain caffeine which is a stimulant. It's perfectly OK to drink tea and coffee as part of a balanced diet – a nice cup of coffee first thing in the morning may well stimulate your mental powers, but be aware that caffeine can leave you restless or jittery. Some people are more affected than others, so make sure you know your limits.

Some studies have found that regular but modest consumption of coffee may help with type 2 diabetes. However, don't take this to mean that you should only drink coffee. It's best to include other fluids, such as water, in your diet.

There's more to tea than ordinary black tea. Alternative teas such as green tea and herbal teas are considered to have lots of beneficial health effects. In fact, green tea has been part of traditional Chinese medicine for centuries. Green tea contains antioxidants, it's thought to stabilize glucose metabolism in diabetes and it may ward off dementia. Green tea comes in many flavors, such as mint or lemon, and there are plenty of herbal teas to choose from, so experiment and find out what you might like.

Fruit juice

Drinking fruit juice is not the same as having a piece of fruit. It often contains as much sugar as sugary fizzy drinks so don't be fooled by the words "no added sugar" on labels. Fruit juice can also stimulate over-eating which is not good for you. It's best to give fruit juice a miss.

Breads and grains

Bread

Wholemeal/whole wheat and wholegrain breads as well as rye bread contain slow-release carbohydrates, and therefore, they are better choices than eating white bread.

I have included an Irish soda bread recipe (p. 50) made with wholemeal/whole wheat flour in this book. The bread keeps fresh for about one day, but it still tastes good the following day if you toast the slices. If you can't manage to eat the whole loaf within a few days, cut it into slices and freeze it.

Breakfast cereals

Most shop-bought breakfast cereals contain high levels of sugar, salt and fat – despite the manufacturers' claims to their healthiness. Porridge oats, however, are a fantastic breakfast cereal. They are believed to keep blood glucose levels low, suppress the appetite, fend off heart disease and boost testosterone levels!

You need to be selective about the kind of porridge oats you buy though. Avoid instant porridge oats as they are bland and resemble wallpaper paste. I use medium steel cut oatmeal. Jumbo oat flakes or rolled oats are also good.

Most shop-bought muesli also contains vast amounts of sugar and salt, but not to worry: you can easily make your own with the help of my muesli recipe (p. 41). Although you will need to start preparing it the night before, don't let this put you off as it will barely take a minute of your time.

Carbohydrates, fat and protein

Our bodies need protein, carbohydrates and fats to function. All three are part of a healthy, balanced diet. Eating too much of any of these or leaving out one of them is not a good idea.

It's important to get enough protein in your diet as it's needed for building and replacing muscle cells in the body. It can also help to keep hunger pangs away. However, eating too much protein may actually cause insulin resistance, so don't overdo it.

Fats are high in calories, so use them sparingly. You don't need to leave them out completely though.

Watch out for serving size and the type of carbohydrates you eat. There are two major categories of carbohydrates: refined carbohydrates and slow-release carbohydrates. Refined carbohydrates are the ones that need to be cut out. These consist of white bread, white pasta, white rice, sugary cereals, cereal bars and, perhaps surprisingly, potatoes.

Refined carbohydrates can be replaced with slow-release carbohydrates such as brown rice, soba noodles, whole wheat pasta, wholemeal/whole wheat or wholegrain bread, steel cut oats/rolled oats and sweet potatoes.

Changing to slow-release carbohydrates will reap considerable benefits as they can help to keep your blood sugar levels on an even keel. They are a good source of fiber and are digested more slowly, which prevents your body from producing too much insulin. Additionally, they provide lots of sustained energy and help you to stay full longer.

If you'd like to treat yourself to a dessert, make sure your main meal hasn't any refined carbohydrates in it and the only slow-release carbohydrates you eat are vegetables. So for example, a main meal of fish, chicken or eggs accompanied by vegetables would be ideal. However, if the dessert is fruit-based, then it's acceptable to have a main course which includes other slow-release carbohydrates.

Dairy

Dairy products contain calcium which helps to keep your bones strong, so it's good to include these in your daily diet.

Butter

Contrary to what many people may think, there is nothing wrong with butter as long as it's eaten in moderation. Since there isn't anything quite like the taste of butter, why deny yourself?

However, since any kind of fat is a concentrated form of calories, try not to eat too much of it.

Cheese

Cheese is a good source of calcium and nutrients, but the downside is that most cheeses are high in fat. Therefore, watch your portion sizes. Since you can only have a little at a time, why not leave out the processed cheeses and buy the best you can afford – and savor it. For example, farmhouse Cheddar, goat's cheese, gorgonzola and feta are great cheeses while the various half-fat cheeses tend to taste like rubber.

Milk

Milk provides good quality protein and a range of vitamins and minerals. Additionally, it appears to have a beneficial effect in reducing blood pressure.

There seem to be different opinions about what kind of milk is best for you: some say you should favor the lower-fat ones; others don't see any problems with having whole milk, provided you have less of it. I prefer to use whole milk, but I always make sure the overall amount in any given day is not too high.

Buttermilk

Genuine buttermilk is the thin liquid left over after cream has been churned into butter. This can be difficult to get hold of unless you live near a farm and the farmer is prepared to sell you some. Luckily supermarkets do sell cultured buttermilk which tastes similar to genuine buttermilk, but is actually made by adding a culture to pasteurized milk.

I like to use buttermilk when I bake soda bread, and my recipe in this book also includes it (p. 50).

Yogurt

I only ever use plain yogurt as the flavored ones tend to be loaded with sugar. I avoid low-fat yogurts like the plague, particularly the zero-fat yogurts, as the fat has been replaced with sugar.

If you like thick creamy Greek yogurt, by all means go for it. Just remember that because of its high fat content you shouldn't over-indulge – a couple of tablespoons over some fruit should suffice.

Desserts and sweets

Sugar/sweeteners

Artificial sweeteners are something I personally tend to avoid. However, if you want to use them, no one will stop you. But if you prefer a natural alternative to, say, aspartame-based sweeteners, try stevia. It's calorie-free and derived from the leaves of the stevia plant.

When making desserts I don't use substitute sugars. I simply put a lot less sugar in the recipe than is usually recommended. If you're wondering whether you could cope with that, let me assure you: as you consume less sugar, your taste buds will eventually adjust to less sweet tastes.

I also use honey. Although it contains more calories than refined sugar, it's metabolized more slowly, which is better for diabetics. I mostly use Manuka honey which has anti-bacterial properties. Even though it's costly, I'd recommend buying the

Active Manuka Honey 15+. Other honeys are fine as well, but a non-blended honey would be preferable.

Chocolate

It's best to avoid milk chocolate and eat 70% dark chocolate instead. It has less sugar and includes nutrients, such as magnesium, potassium and iron. Luckily, my husband has always preferred dark chocolate so he didn't have to get used to its flavor. If, however, you do struggle with this, remember that as your eating habits become healthier, your body learns not to crave unhealthier options. Also, if plain dark chocolate doesn't really appeal to you, try some which have added flavors, like raspberries or orange.

Desserts

If possible, eat desserts straight after a meal. If they are eaten on their own, they can cause your blood sugar levels to spike. (Read more about refined and slow-release carbohydrates in the Carbohydrates, fat and protein section, p. 13).

Most of the desserts in this book are fruit-based. If this seems boring, all I can say is: don't dismiss them out of hand! Fruit can be absolutely delicious when baked with a little honey and spice. In fact, the baking process can significantly alter the texture and flavor of the fruit.

One of my husband's favorite desserts is apple crumble. On finding out that he was a diabetic this was one of the first things he mourned. All was not lost, however. I now use eating apples instead of cooking apples when I make apple crumble, or indeed any apple desserts. While the cooking apples can be quite sour and cry out for sugar, eating apples are naturally sweeter. I always use the sweetest eating apples I can lay my hands on – varieties such as Pink Lady, Gala or Red Delicious are excellent for these recipes. All my children have a sweet tooth, but none of them have ever complained that the desserts aren't sweet enough.

When I use or eat apples, I don't peel them as the skin is where most of the vitamin C and fiber can be found. Not peeling them also saves a little time when you're preparing your meal.

Some people feel that the fruit desserts included in this eating plan don't sit right without a little cream. If you are one of these individuals, feel free to add a few tablespoons of lower-fat variety of cream (for example, single cream in the UK and half-and-half or light cream in the US).

I don't believe in being limiting, so in addition to the fruit-based desserts, I have also included an indulgent, yet light, Chocolate orange mousse recipe (p. 88) which is a perfect way to end a meal.

Fruit and vegetables

Fruit contains high levels of vitamins and minerals which are needed for a healthy body. Fruit juice, however, isn't the same as having a piece of fruit (see the Fruit juice section on p. 12 for more details).

Generally speaking, all the different kinds of fruit are good for you. For example, apples are great snacks as they are so easy to carry with you and berries are wonderful as they tend to be low in sugar and rich in antioxidants. However, there are some fruits that diabetics need to watch out for:

Bananas, although a good source of potassium, contain too much sugar when they are over-ripe. Avoid eating them if they have brown spots on their skin.

Mangos can also be too sweet, so only eat them occasionally.

Fresh *figs* are great for diabetics, but avoid the dried ones as they are way too sugary.

Vegetables

Always include plenty of fresh vegetables as part of your eating plan. They contain high levels of vitamins and minerals.

I occasionally use frozen vegetables – and I don't feel like I'm cheating when I do this! Due to modern freezing techniques, it would seem that frozen vegetables (in most cases anyway) have a similar nutritional content to fresh ones.

Potatoes

Potatoes do not contain slow-release carbohydrates, so I have omitted them from this eating plan. When potatoes would normally be included in a meal, I use sweet potatoes instead. For example, in this book there's a shepherd's pie recipe (p. 78). When I first made this dish, I didn't know how my husband Anthony would react. It turned out that he actually preferred it to the traditional shepherd's pie – so, I named the recipe Anthony's shepherd's pie.

If you must eat potatoes, make sure they are new potatoes. Chips/ fries and roast potatoes are out of the question, as are baked jacket potatoes. Baked potatoes are generally seen as a healthy meal option as they are low in fat and high in fiber. However, they are rather large and this can cause a sugar surge.

New potatoes have a much milder effect on blood sugar balance. However, you still need to be a little careful: if you do choose to eat new potatoes, eat them in moderation alongside meat or fish and non-starchy vegetables, such as spinach, sprouts, spring greens, pak choi/bok choy, broccoli and cauliflower. Avoid combining them with peas, sweet potatoes, parsnips and Jerusalem artichokes.

Mushrooms

Mushrooms tend to be prepared by frying them in butter – in fact, you might think they virtually scream out for butter – but it's not necessary to fry them. I sometimes boil them instead. Most mushrooms can also be eaten without cooking.

Meat, fish and eggs

Meat, fish and eggs contain protein which the body needs for building and replacing muscle cells. It's best to eat them in moderation as too much protein may lead to insulin resistance.

Meat

Choose meats and cuts that are not excessively fatty. For example, chicken breast is better than pork belly.

If you love bacon – indeed, I have even known vegetarians who are magically drawn to the smell of bacon cooking – you don't have to cut it out of your diet completely. (I'd hate to think you would miss out on one of life's pleasures!) Go for medallions which have no unnecessary fat or cut off any excess fat before you cook the rashers. Don't be tempted by streaky bacon and lardons as they are too fatty.

Fish

Fish is a great source of protein and other nutrients. It can also be easier to digest than meat.

I have included some fish recipes in this book. If you don't eat fish, you can make the dishes by using chicken instead.

Eggs

Eggs are an amazing convenience food. Not only do they contain many vitamins and minerals, they also satisfy your appetite. When buying your eggs, go for free-range, or better still, organic eggs.

All eggs used in the recipes are large.

Nuts and seeds

Nuts are a concentrated form of protein and monounsaturated fats and they are thought to lower cholesterol. Almonds, walnuts and pine nuts are part of this eating plan. You can also eat macadamia nuts, brazil nuts, pecans, pistachios and hazelnuts. However, make sure you avoid salted nuts of any variety.

I also add sesame seeds to many dishes as they have a great taste and are rich in minerals.

Peanuts – and peanut butter – are best avoided. They are actually not nuts at all, but legumes. And like all legumes, they contain about the same amount of protein as starch. Some people find this indigestible.

Packed lunches

Traditionally a packed lunch for most people means sandwiches. But it's not a good idea to have bread every single day. Try to vary what you eat.

When I plan packed lunches, I try to avoid ingredients that won't travel well or become smelly – fish comes to mind. However, fish as part of a packed lunch works well as long as it's stored in an air-tight container and you are able to pop your lunchbox in a fridge at work.

Pizza

Who says you can't eat pizza? The greasy goo found in a ready-made or take-out pizza bears no resemblance to a homemade pizza. I cook pizza when I'm not in the mood to make a full-blown meal. Our family often munch these on the sofa while watching TV.

I stick to cheese and tomato as this makes for an easy meal. I use 100% concentrated tomato purée for the topping as it's super quick to use. Although this may seem like a bit of a cheat, don't feel guilty: it's not bad for you – and it's OK to take some shortcuts every now and then!

Snacks

Diabetics not only have to think about what to eat, but also when and how often to eat. Eating regularly means your body is more able to regulate blood sugar levels. Aim to eat six times a day: ideally three meals and three snacks. If you leave too long a gap between meals you may become overly hungry, which may lead to eating larger meals. Try not to allow more than 2 ½ hours between a snack or meal.

Snacks are important as they prevent the tidal wave of hunger before your next meal. Ideally, the morning snack should be taken a couple of hours after breakfast. The first afternoon snack should be eaten a couple of hours after lunch and the second afternoon/evening snack a couple of hours before dinner. *Never miss a snack or meal.* At the end of the day, if you are still feeling peckish, don't go to bed hungry – allow yourself an extra snack. A couple of oat cookies (p. 66) usually does the trick.

In this book I have suggested different kinds of snacks: all are quick and easy to eat, such as a piece of fruit, a handful of nuts and raisins, or an oat cookie (p. 66). Any of these should be enough to tide you over to the next meal.

A cup of chicken stock is also used as a snack. This is a tasty thin soup and it really hits the mark. My mum used to serve big steaming bowls of this stuff and swore that it would "clear a cold and soothe a sore throat"!

Spices, herbs and condiments

Herbs and spices

All herbs and spices included in the recipes have health benefits. But the two most beneficial spices are curry leaves and cinnamon. I always include curry leaves in any kind of curry or stew. Curry leaves don't taste of 'curry' even though the name implies that.

They have a smoky lemony flavor that complements other spices. But it's not just the taste that is appealing. Curry leaves are thought to slow down the rate at which starch is converted to glucose, which is helpful for diabetics.

Cinnamon is a beautifully fragrant spice. It's incredibly versatile and can be used in curries as well as desserts. Cinnamon may reduce blood pressure as well as help with glucose control.

Salt

When you cook yourself and know what's in your food, it's easier to keep track of how much salt you're taking in. Avoid using salt excessively or adding more salt to your food at the table. I have found that by using sea salt crystals in my cooking I instinctively use less salt.

Vinegar

Vinegar is thought to prevent blood sugar levels from spiking and, when used regularly, it may also help you to lose weight. Vinegar is a wonderful addition to gravies as it adds a sweet-sharp dimension to them, mingling beautifully with the richness of meat juices.

About measurements

The measurements in the book are in metric units, imperial units and US cup measures. The metric units are given first, the imperial units follow in brackets and the US cup measures follow these.

Please note that the conversions are approximations and have been rounded either up or down.

A teaspoon (tsp) is 5 ml and a tablespoon (tbsp) is 15 ml. 3 teaspoons equal 1 tablespoon. Often the spoons used in everyday life are smaller than these. Therefore, it's best to use measures that are specifically meant for cooking purposes. Also, always use level measures.

EATING PLAN

Day 1

Breakfast
Porridge (p. 39)

Morning snack
1 pear

Lunch
Nutty pasta (p. 48)

Afternoon snack
A couple of oat cookies (p. 66)

Late afternoon snack
A couple of red plums or a handful of grapes

Dinner
Saucy trout (p. 72)
Baked apples (p. 87)

Day 2

Breakfast
Sesame bananas (p. 40)

Morning snack
A handful of walnuts and raisins

Lunch
A couple of Mum's Irish soda bread slices (p. 50)
topped with Grand guacamole (p. 47)

Afternoon snack
A handful of berries
(for example, blueberries, blackberries and/or raspberries)

Late afternoon snack
1 apple

Dinner
Lemon chicken (p. 74)
Chocolate orange mousse (p. 88)

Day 3

Breakfast
Muesli (p. 41)

Morning snack
1 portion of chicken stock (p. 65)

Lunch
Chunky salmon (p. 52)

Afternoon snack
1 pear

Late afternoon snack
A handful of sesame seeds and sunflower seeds

Dinner
Goat's cheese omelette (p. 76)
Apple crumble (p. 90)

Day 4

Breakfast
Strawberry and banana smoothie (p. 42)

Morning snack
A couple of red plums or a handful of grapes

Lunch
Aubergine/eggplant pâté on toast (p. 54)

Afternoon snack
1 portion of chicken stock (p. 65)

Late afternoon snack
1 apple

Dinner
Anthony's shepherd's pie (p. 78)
Creamy custard (p. 92)

Day 5

Breakfast
Porridge (p. 39)

Morning snack
1 apple

Lunch
Noodly tuna (p. 56)

Afternoon snack
A handful of sesame seeds and sunflower seeds

Late afternoon snack
A couple of red plums or a handful of grapes

Dinner
Quick pizza (p. 80)
Cinnamon pears (p. 94)

Day 6

Breakfast
Muesli (p. 41)

Morning snack
A handful of walnuts and raisins

Lunch
Ratatouille (p. 58)

Afternoon snack
1 banana

Late afternoon snack
A couple of red plums or a handful of grapes

Dinner
Pesto linguine (p. 71)
Baked goat's cheese figs (p. 95)

Day 7

Breakfast
Pineapple fool (p. 43)

Morning snack
1 banana

Lunch
Sweet potato soup (p. 60)

Afternoon snack
A couple of oat cookies (p. 66)

Late afternoon snack
A handful of berries
(for example, blueberries, blackberries and/or raspberries)

Dinner
Chicken and green bean curry (p. 82)
Apple and raisin bake (p. 96)

BREAKFAST
RECIPES

Porridge

Serves 2

450 ml (16 fl oz) 2 cups water

120 g (4 oz) 1 ¼ cups oats

A pinch of sea salt

1 banana

Up to 60 ml (2 fl oz) ¼ cup milk for serving (optional)

1. Put the water into a saucepan and bring to the boil (or boil the water in a kettle and pour it into the saucepan).

2. Stir in the oats and cook the porridge slightly under boiling point for about 3 minutes (or for longer if the cooking instructions on the oats packet say so). Stir the porridge every now and then.

3. Divide the porridge between two bowls and add salt to taste. Don't worry if the porridge appears watery, it will thicken to the right consistency in a few minutes.

4. Chop the banana and add it to the bowls. If you like to eat your porridge with milk, add that too.

Sesame bananas

Serves 2

2 bananas
250 ml (8 fl oz) 1 cup plain yogurt
A handful of sesame seeds

1. Chop the bananas and put them into two bowls.

2. Pour the yogurt over the bananas.

3. Sprinkle the sesame seeds on top.

Muesli

Serves 2

You need to start preparing this muesli the night before. Don't be alarmed by this though: it won't take long!

1 tbsp oats

4 tbsp water

6 tbsp plain yogurt

2 ripe apples

2 tsp lemon juice

2 tsp chopped walnuts

2 tsp raisins

Night before:
1. Put the oats and water into a bowl and mix.

2. Stir in the yogurt.

3. Cover the bowl and place it in a fridge overnight.

Next morning:
1. Take the muesli bowl out of the fridge.

2. Coarsely grate the apples and stir into the oats mixture.

3. Mix in the lemon juice.

4. Divide the muesli between two bowls and scatter the chopped walnuts and raisins on top.

Strawberry and banana smoothie

Serves 2

2 bananas

120 g (4 oz) ¾ cup strawberries

250 ml (8 fl oz) 1 cup plain yogurt

60 ml (2 fl oz) ¼ cup water

3 ice cubes

1. Place all the ingredients in a blender and blend until the mixture is smooth.

2. Pour the smoothie into two glasses and serve.

Pineapple fool

Serves 2

180 g (6 oz) 1 cup fresh pineapple
250 g (8 fl oz) 1 cup plain yogurt
2 tsp sesame seeds

1. Chop the pineapple into small pieces and put them into a bowl.

2. Pour the yogurt over the pineapple pieces and mix.

3. Divide the mixture between two serving bowls and sprinkle the sesame seeds on top.

LUNCH
RECIPES

Grand guacamole

Serves 2

2 small ripe avocados

1 small green pepper/bell pepper

Juice of a lime

4 tbsp extra virgin olive oil

½ tsp sea salt

½ tsp cayenne pepper

A handful of fresh coriander/cilantro

4-6 spring onions/scallions

60 g (2 oz) hard cheese (for example, Cheddar)

1. Cut the avocados in half lengthways and twist like a Rubik's Cube to open them. Remove the stone. Scoop out the avocado flesh, put it into a bowl and mash roughly with a fork.

2. Coarsely chop the green pepper/bell pepper and add to the mashed avocado.

3. Add the lime juice, olive oil, salt, cayenne pepper and coriander/cilantro.

4. Tip the mixture into a blender and blend for 20-30 seconds.

5 Chop the spring onions/scallions finely and stir into the mixture.

6. Cut two doorstop slices of Mum's Irish soda bread (p. 50) and spread the guacamole generously on them. Grate the cheese and sprinkle it on top of the guacamole.

Nutty pasta

Serves 2

Water for boiling the pasta and mushrooms
A pinch of sea salt
120 g (4 oz) whole wheat pasta
1 small green pepper/bell pepper
240 g (9 oz) 3 cups mushrooms
½ tsp nutmeg
60 ml (2 fl oz) ¼ cup sour cream
A dash of ground black pepper
120 g (4 oz) 1 cup chopped walnuts

1. Fill a large saucepan with water and bring it to the boil (or boil the water in a kettle and pour it into the saucepan). Add a pinch of salt.

2. Add the pasta and cook until it's al dente (tender but firm to the bite).

3. While the pasta is cooking, finely chop the green pepper/bell pepper and set aside.

4. Roughly chop the mushrooms.

5. Take another saucepan, fill it with water and bring it to the boil (or use a kettle to boil the water). Add the mushrooms and boil them for about 10 minutes. If you prefer to eat your mushrooms raw, set the mushrooms aside until they are needed.

6. When the pasta is ready, drain it and leave to cool in the saucepan while you're preparing the rest of the dish.

7. When the mushrooms are cooked, drain them and sprinkle with some nutmeg. Set aside.

8. Take a small bowl and mix together the sour cream and black pepper in it.

9. Now combine the different elements: mix in the mushrooms, chopped green pepper/bell pepper and walnuts to the pasta, and finally stir in the sour cream.

Mum's Irish soda bread

This bread goes wonderfully with Grand guacamole (p. 47). Make the bread first and prepare the guacamole while the bread is cooling.

1 tbsp unsalted butter for greasing the baking tray

450 g (16 oz) 3 cups wholemeal/whole wheat flour + extra for flouring the work surface

½ tsp sea salt

2 tsp bicarbonate of soda/baking soda

500 ml (16 fl oz) 2 cups buttermilk*

1 tbsp honey

2 tbsp oats

1. Pre-heat the oven to 200C/400F/gas mark 6.

2. Grease a baking tray with butter (or line the tray with non-stick baking parchment).

3. Place the flour, salt and soda in a bowl, give them a quick stir and make a well in the middle.

4. Pour in a third of the buttermilk and mix it in with your hands. As you work the mixture, it will be very floury at this stage.

5. Add the honey and another third of the buttermilk, and mix again with your hands.

6. Mix in the remaining buttermilk slowly. At this point the dough may feel quite wet.

7. Sprinkle some flour on a work surface and turn the wettish dough out onto it.

8. Knead the dough for a minute. As you start doing this, you will find that the dough very quickly becomes soft and elastic.

9. Form the dough into a round shape and place it onto the baking tray.

10. Cut a deep cross into the dough with a knife – it should look as though the bread is cut into quarters – and sprinkle the oats over the bread.

11. Put the bread in the oven and bake for 40-45 minutes.

12. When it's time to take the bread out of the oven, use a spatula or a knife to lift the bread (it should come away from the baking tray quite easily). Tap the bread on the underside. If it has a hollow sound, it's done.

13. Keep the bread wrapped in a cloth until you're ready to eat it.

* Buttermilk substitution

If you are unable to obtain buttermilk, mix together 125 ml (4 fl oz) ½ cup of whole milk and 500 ml (16 fl oz) 2 cups of plain yogurt, and use this in the same way you'd use the buttermilk in the recipe. You will also need to rub 60 g (2 oz) ½ stick of butter into the dry ingredients before you start adding the liquid.

Chunky salmon

Serves 2

2 x 140-180 g (5-6 oz) salmon fillets*
2 tsp unsalted butter
A handful of coarsely chopped dill
8 spring onions/scallions
120 g (4 oz) ½ cup frozen or canned chickpeas**
120 g (4 oz) ½ cup frozen or fresh peas
120 g (4 oz) ½ cup frozen, canned or fresh sweet corn

Dressing
Juice of a lemon
1 tbsp extra virgin olive oil
A pinch of sea salt
A dash of ground black pepper

1. Pre-heat the oven to 180C/350F/gas mark 4.

2. Take two pieces of silver foil and place a salmon fillet in the middle of each piece. Put a teaspoon of butter on top of each fillet and wrap them in the foil.

3. Bake the salmon in the oven for about 15 minutes.

4. While the salmon is cooking, roughly chop the dill and spring onions/scallions. Set them aside.

5. Boil the chickpeas, peas and sweet corn for 3-5 minutes and set them aside.

6. To make the dressing, squeeze the juice of one lemon into a screw-top jar. Add the olive oil, salt and pepper, then fasten the lid and shake vigorously until the dressing is thoroughly blended.

7. When the salmon fillets are ready, break them up and place onto serving plates (or if you're planning to take a packed lunch with you, put the salmon pieces into air-tight containers).

8. Add the chickpeas, sweet corn, peas, dill and spring onions/ scallions on top of the salmon and pour over the dressing.

* Fish substitution

If you don't eat fish, replace the salmon with chicken breasts and bake for additional 10-15 minutes.

** Chickpea substitution

In this recipe I have used frozen chickpeas for convenience. If you are thinking of using canned chickpeas, it's best to buy jars of ready-cooked chickpeas preserved in salt, without artificial preservatives. You can also use dried chickpeas, but this will require a lot of boiling first to soften them.

Aubergine/eggplant pâté on toast

Serves 2

You will need some wholemeal/whole wheat bread or Mum's Irish soda bread (p. 50) to go with this pâté. If you'd like to bake your own bread, start by doing that.

2 small aubergines/eggplants

4 tbsp extra virgin olive oil

Juice of a lemon

A pinch of sea salt

A dash of ground black pepper

2 cloves garlic

1. Pre-heat the oven to 180C/350F/gas mark 4 and line an oven tray with non-stick baking parchment.

2. Score slits across the aubergines/eggplants with a sharp knife, place them on the oven tray and bake for 20-30 minutes.

3. When the aubergines/eggplants are cooked, take them out of the oven and leave to cool for about 5 minutes.

4. Slice each aubergine/eggplant in half, gouge out the flesh and put it into a blender.

5. Add the olive oil, lemon juice, salt, pepper and garlic cloves, and blend for about 20 seconds on a low setting.

6. Place the pâté in a fridge for at least a couple of hours.

7. When you are ready to use the pâté, serve it on toasted wholemeal/whole wheat bread or Mum's Irish soda bread. If you're planning to take a packed lunch with you, wait for the toast to go cold before making your sandwich and putting it in your lunchbox.

Noodly tuna

Serves 2

2 x 140-180 g (5-6 oz) tuna steaks*

2 tsp unsalted butter

120 g (4 oz) soba noodles

Water for boiling the noodles

A pinch of sea salt

120 g (4 oz) 1 ½ cups mushrooms

1 green pepper/bell pepper

2 tbsp extra virgin olive oil

2 tbsp apple cider vinegar

125 ml (4 fl oz) ½ cup of chicken stock (see the recipe on p. 65 or use chicken stock cubes/bouillon cubes to make the stock)

1. Pre-heat the oven to 180C/350F/gas mark 4.

2. Take two pieces of silver foil and place a tuna steak in the middle of each piece. Put a teaspoon of butter on top of each steak and wrap them in the foil.

3. Bake the tuna fillets in the oven for 15-20 minutes.

4. While the tuna is in the oven, cook the noodles: fill a saucepan with water and bring it to the boil (you can also use a kettle to boil the water). Place the noodles in the boiling water, add a pinch of salt and boil for as long as instructed on the packet.

5. Drain the noodles and divide them between two plates (or airtight containers if you're making a packed lunch).

6. When the tuna is ready, take it out of the oven, break it into pieces and set them aside for the time being.

7. Roughly chop the mushrooms and the green pepper/bell pepper.

8. Heat the oil in a frying pan. Add the mushrooms and peppers into the pan and fry for about 5 minutes.

9. Add the apple cider vinegar and chicken stock into the pan and continue to heat for a few more minutes.

10. Put the tuna and the vegetables over the noodles, and pour any juices over them.

* Substitutions

If you don't want to use tuna steaks, you can use canned tuna in spring water or brine. Instead of baking the tuna, skip Steps 2 and 3, and warm it up in a microwave for a minute or two.

Chicken breasts can also be used instead of tuna steaks – this will require 10-15 minutes more cooking time.

Ratatouille

Serves 2

3 cloves garlic

1 red onion

1 red pepper/bell pepper

4 small courgettes/zucchinis

1 small aubergine/eggplant

2 big tomatoes

4 tbsp olive oil

680 ml (24 fl oz) 3 cups passata

A pinch of sea salt

A dash of ground black pepper

2 tbsp apple cider vinegar

120 g (4 oz) grated hard cheese (for example, Cheddar)

1. Finely chop the garlic. Cut the onion into thick rings, the red pepper/bell pepper into chunky strips, and the courgettes/zucchinis and aubergine/eggplant into large chunks. There's no need to chop the tomatoes if you don't want to as they will disintegrate during the cooking process.

2. Heat the olive oil in a large saucepan. Fry the garlic for a couple of minutes on a medium heat, stirring occasionally.

3. Stir in the onion and red peppers/bell peppers and fry them until they are starting to soften.

4. Stir in the courgettes/zucchinis and aubergine/eggplant and fry them for a few minutes.

5. Add the tomatoes and fry them for another few minutes. Keep stirring the vegetables every now and then.

6. Stir in the tomato passata, salt, black pepper and vinegar. Wait until the liquid starts to bubble. Then turn the heat to its lowest setting, put a lid on the pan and leave to cook for 45-60 minutes. Check and stir the ratatouille occasionally.

7. Divide the ratatouille between two plates (or air-tight containers if you're making a packed lunch). Grate some cheese and sprinkle it on top.

Sweet potato soup

Serves 4-6

3-4 large sweet potatoes

1 red onion

4 tbsp olive oil

1 litre (1 ¾ pt) 4 cups water

180 g (6 oz) bacon medallions/non-fatty bacon

3 tbsp apple cider vinegar

A pinch of sea salt

A dash of ground black pepper

1. Peel and chop the sweet potatoes into chunks and set aside.

2. Finely chop the red onion.

3. Heat the olive oil in a large saucepan and fry the onions until they soften. Stir every now and then.

4. Stir in the chunks of sweet potato and cook them for approximately 3 minutes.

5. Add the water and increase the heat to bring the water to the boil.

6. Turn down the heat and let the soup simmer for 10-15 minutes or until the sweet potato chunks are tender but not mushy.

7. While the soup is simmering, cut the bacon into small pieces and pop them in a frying pan on a low heat. You don't need to add any oil as the bacon is fatty enough.

8. When the sweet potatoes have cooked, turn off the heat and pour the soup into a blender. Blend on a low speed for about a minute.

9. Add the apple cider vinegar, salt and pepper to the soup and blend for further 30 seconds.

10. Pour the soup into bowls and sprinkle the fried bacon pieces on top.

SNACK
RECIPES

Chicken stock

Makes 2 snack portions

1 big onion

Leftover chicken carcass and bones (for example from Lemon chicken, p. 74)

1 litre (1 ¾ pt) 4 cups water

A pinch of sea salt

A dash of ground black pepper

1. Peel and chop the onion.

2. Place all the ingredients in a large saucepan.

3. Bring the water to the boil, then simmer the stock for 30 minutes. This should reduce the amount of liquid down to about 300 ml (10 fl oz) 1 ¼ cups.

4. Sieve the stock. If you don't want to drink all of the stock immediately, you can store it in a fridge overnight or freeze it for later use.

Oat cookies

Makes about 12 cookies

1 tsp unsalted butter for greasing trays + 1 tsp for the cookie dough

½ tsp sea salt

125 ml (4 fl oz) ½ cup boiling water

120 g (4 oz) 1 ¼ cups oats

60 g (2 oz) 7 tbsp wholemeal/whole wheat flour for flouring the work surface

1. Pre-heat the oven to 200C /400F/gas mark 6.

2. Grease 1-2 baking trays with some butter (or line the trays with non-stick baking parchment).

3. Put 1 teaspoon of butter and ½ teaspoon of salt into a mixing bowl.

4. Boil the water and pour it into the bowl. Mix and wait for the butter to melt.

5. Add the oats and mix thoroughly. Leave the dough to stand for a couple of minutes. The dough will be quite wet.

6. Sprinkle the flour onto a work surface and place the dough on it.

7. Cut the dough into quarters and thinly roll out each piece with a rolling pin. Make sure you flour the rolling pin first so the dough doesn't stick to it.

8. Cut the rolled-out piece into 3 shapes of your choice and place them on the baking tray. Do the same with the rest of the dough pieces.

9. Bake the cookies for about 10 minutes or until they are slightly golden. Serve the cookies on the day you make them or store them in an air-tight cookie jar and eat them the following day.

DINNER
RECIPES

Pesto linguine

Serves 4

Water for boiling the linguine

A pinch of sea salt

240 g (8 oz) wholemeal/whole wheat linguine

120 g (6 oz) ¾ cup pine nuts (or pistachios)

6 tomatoes

A dash of ground black pepper

2 large handfuls of fresh basil leaves

6 tbsp extra virgin olive oil

60 g (2 oz) Parmesan or Pecorino (or some other hard cheese of your choice)

1. Fill a large saucepan with water, add the salt and bring the water to the boil.

2. Add the linguine and cook until it's al dente (tender but firm to the bite)

3. While the linguine is boiling, chop the tomatoes.

4. Put the tomatoes, pine nuts, black pepper, basil, olive oil and cheese into a blender and blend on a low setting for 10-15 seconds.

5. When the linguine is ready, drain it, put it back into the saucepan and pour the pesto over it. Serve immediately.

Saucy trout

Serves 4

Water for poaching the trout and boiling the peas

6 tbsp apple cider vinegar

2 bay leaves

12 black peppercorns

4 x 140-180 g (5-6 oz) trout fillets*

120 g (4 oz) ¾ cup fresh or frozen peas

120 g (4 oz) 1 ½ cups fresh or frozen mange tout/snap peas

A handful of fresh mint

Almond sauce

1 tbsp chopped fresh parsley (or some dried parsley)

60 g (2 oz) ½ stick unsalted butter

60 ml (2 fl oz) ¼ cup double cream/heavy cream

A pinch of sea salt

A dash of ground black pepper

4 tbsp flaked almonds

1. Fill a large saucepan with water and mix the vinegar into it. Bring the water to the boil.

2. Add the bay leaves and peppercorns into the saucepan.

3. Place the trout fillets into the boiling water and allow them to simmer for 12-15 minutes or until they are cooked.

4. While the trout is cooking, take another saucepan and prepare the vegetables: boil the peas and mange tout/snap peas for a few minutes.

5. While the peas and mange tout/snap peas are boiling, coarsely chop the mint.

6. Drain peas and mange tout/snap peas and put them back into the saucepan. Sprinkle the mint on top. Set the saucepan aside.

7. When the trout fillets are cooked, drain them, peel the skins off and carefully lift the flesh from the bones, removing any small bones you may come across. Let the trout rest in the saucepan while you make the almond sauce.

8. Roughly chop the parsley and set aside.

9. Now make the sauce: take a small saucepan and melt the butter in it.

10. Stir in the cream, salt and pepper. Turn down the heat and wait for the sauce to heat through. When it comes to the boil, take it off the heat.

11. Divide the trout and peas between four plates. Pour the sauce over the trout and sprinkle the almond flakes and chopped parsley on top.

* Fish substitution

If you do not eat fish, you can use chicken breasts instead. The cooking time for chicken would be 10-15 minutes longer.

Lemon chicken

Serves 4

This lemon chicken is not only a wonderful dinner, but its remnants can be used to make a chicken stock snack (p. 65) – so don't discard the carcass and the bones!

Approximately 1.8 kg (4 lb) free range or organic chicken

2 tsp unsalted butter

1 lemon

4 cloves

3 tbsp apple cider vinegar

300 ml (10 fl oz) 1 ¼ cups chicken stock (see the recipe on p. 65 or use chicken stock cubes/bouillon cubes to make the stock)

240 g (8 oz) 3 ½ cups pak choi/bok choy/Chinese cabbage

1. Check the chicken wrapping for cooking instructions. Usually 1.8 kg (4 lb) chicken takes about 1 ½ - 1 ¾ hours to cook at 180C/350F/gas mark 4. However, if the instructions on the packet suggest something different, follow them.

2. Pre-heat the oven to the required temperature.

3. Put the chicken into a roasting tray and smear 1 teaspoon of butter over the breast.

4. Cut the lemon in half. Place one half inside the chicken with 1 teaspoon of butter and the cloves.

5. Squeeze the juice of the other lemon half over the chicken breast and legs.

6. Put the chicken in the oven and cook according to the instructions on the wrapping.

7. When you think the chicken is cooked, insert a skewer into it to make sure the juices are running clear. If there is any pinkness, put the chicken back in the oven.

8. When the chicken is cooked, take it out of the oven and tip away the fat from the baking tray – you will be left with the chicken juices.

9. Pour the chicken juices into a saucepan. Scrape any crusty roasted bits from the roasting tray and add them into the saucepan as well. Set the chicken aside to rest.

10. Add the apple cider vinegar and the additional stock into the saucepan.

11. Roughly chop the pak choi/bok choy/Chinese cabbage and place the pieces in the saucepan.

12. Heat the saucepan, and once the liquid comes to the boil, let it simmer for a few minutes. The softer parts of the pak choi/bok choy/Chinese cabbage will wilt while the harder parts will retain some crispiness.

13. Carve the chicken and serve with the pak choi/bok choy/Chinese cabbage gravy.

Goat's cheese omelette

Serves 2

120 g (4 oz) 1 ½ cups mushrooms
Water for boiling the mushrooms
120 g (4 oz) soft goat's cheese
6 large eggs at room temperature
60 g (2 oz) ½ stick unsalted butter
A pinch of sea salt
A dash of ground black pepper

1. Slice the mushrooms.

2. Fill a saucepan with water and bring to the boil (or use a kettle to boil the water). Put the mushrooms into the saucepan and boil for 5 minutes. If you prefer to eat your mushrooms raw, you can skip this and the next stage.

3. Take the mushrooms out of the saucepan and leave them in a colander to drain.

4. Cut the goat's cheese into small pieces and set them aside for the time being.

5. Break the eggs into a bowl and whisk them enough to combine the whites and the yolks.

6. Take a large frying pan and heat the butter in it. As the butter melts, it will start to bubble and foam. When the foam has died down a little, pour in the eggs and shake the pan to distribute them evenly.

7. Cook the omelette for approximately 20 seconds.

8. Add the goat's cheese and mushrooms on top of the omelette and continue cooking. When only a little of the omelette appears unset in the centre, it's done.

9. Take the frying pan off the heat and use a spatula to lift the omelette onto a plate. Cut it into two portions and serve immediately.

Anthony's shepherd's pie

Serves 4-5

5 large sweet potatoes

Water for boiling the sweet potatoes

2 cloves garlic

10 mushrooms

1 onion

3 tbsp olive oil

240 g (8 oz) lean minced/ground lamb

225 ml (8 fl oz) 1 cup chicken stock (see the recipe on p. 65 or use chicken stock cubes/bouillon cubes to make the stock)

A pinch of salt

A dash of ground black pepper

1. Pre-heat the oven to 200C/400F/gas mark 6.

2. Peel the sweet potatoes and chop them into chunks.

3. Take a large saucepan, fill it with water and bring it to the boil (or use a kettle to boil the water). Add the sweet potatoes into the saucepan and boil them until they are tender.

4. While the sweet potatoes are boiling, chop the garlic, onion and mushrooms.

5. Take a large frying pan and heat the olive oil in it.

6. Fry the garlic on a low heat for a couple of minutes, stirring every now and then.

7. Stir in the onions and mushrooms and fry them until the onions have softened.

8. Add the minced/ground lamb and any juices left in the packet. Give the mixture a good stir, breaking up the texture. Fry the mixture for 4-5 minutes and stir occasionally.

9. Stir in the stock. Cook for a few more minutes and then take the pan off the heat. The mince may only be partially cooked at this point, but that doesn't matter as it will be cooked further in the oven.

10. Take a high-sided oven-proof dish and spoon the minced/ground lamb mixture, including any excess liquid, into it.

11. When the sweet potatoes are tender, drain and mash them. Mix in the salt and black pepper.

12. Spread the mash over the minced/ground lamb mixture and place the dish in the oven for 20-30 minutes. The shepherd's pie is ready when the mash starts to brown a little. Serve immediately.

Quick pizza

Makes 6 large pizzas or 12 small ones

1 tbsp unsalted butter for greasing baking trays

360 g (12 oz) hard cheese (for example, Cheddar) or mozzarella

450 g (16 oz) 3 cups wholemeal/whole wheat flour + extra 5 tbsp for flouring the work surface

A pinch of sea salt

370 ml (12 fl oz) 1 ½ cups lukewarm water

300 g (10 oz) 1 ¼ cups tomato purée

1. Pre-heat the oven to 230C/450F/gas mark 8.

2. Grease 2-3 baking trays with butter (or line the trays with non-stick baking parchment).

3. Grate the cheese and set it aside for later.

4. Put the flour into a bowl, add the salt and stir.

5. Add the water, and as you do so, mix the dough with your hands. The dough will become stretchy. If you find that your dough is too wet, add more flour.

6. Flour your work surface and place the dough onto it. Cut the dough into six pieces and shape them into six balls with your hands (or twelve balls if you want to make small pizzas).

7. Take the first ball of dough and roll it out with a rolling pin. Make the pizza base as thin as possible. You don't have to make it into a particular shape (like a round or square) – as long as the pizza base fits on a baking tray, it's fine. Remember to flour your

rolling pin to avoid the dough sticking to it. Also, keep turning over the dough so that it doesn't stick to the surface. Add more flour if needed.

8. To lift the pizza base onto the baking tray, roll it around the rolling pin and unfurl it onto the baking tray.

9. Repeat this process with the rest of the dough balls.

10. Once the pizza bases are on the baking trays, spread the tomato purée on them and sprinkle the cheese on top.

11. Bake the pizzas for about 5 minutes or until the cheese has melted.

Chicken and green bean curry

Serves 6

6 chicken breasts

6 tbsp water

1 tsp ground mustard

1 tsp ground cumin

1 tsp ground cinnamon

2 tsp fresh root ginger (or some ground ginger)

½ tsp ground turmeric

15 dried or fresh curry leaves

2 cloves garlic

1 small onion

2 fresh green chillies

2 tbsp olive oil

120 g (4 oz) ¾ cup green beans

500 ml (16 fl oz) 2 cups plain yogurt

1. Cut the chicken breasts into small pieces and place them in a large bowl.

2. Put the water, mustard, cumin, cinnamon, ginger, turmeric and curry leaves into a blender or an electric chopper and blitz them until you have a grainy paste. You can also do this with the help of a pestle and mortar.

3. Coat the chicken pieces with the spicy paste.

4. Cover the chicken and place it in the fridge for at least 2 hours.

5. When you are ready to make the curry, chop the garlic, onion and chillies.

6. Heat the oil in a large frying pan.

7. Fry the garlic for a couple of minutes, stirring occasionally.

8. Stir in the onion and chillies, and fry them for another minute. Stir every now and then.

9. Stir in the marinated chicken and cook the curry until the juices in the pan start to bubble. Then turn down the heat and cook for 10 minutes. If it looks like the curry is getting too dry, add some water.

10. Stir in the green beans and leave the curry to simmer for 25 minutes. Stir occasionally and check that the curry doesn't dry out.

11. Just before you're ready to serve the curry, stir in the yogurt and cook gently for another 30 seconds. (If you cook it for longer, the yogurt may curdle.) Serve immediately.

DESSERT
RECIPES

Baked apples

Serves 6

6 large eating apples

6 tsp chopped walnuts

6 tsp raisins

6 tsp honey

1. Pre-heat the oven to 180C/350C/gas mark 4.

2. De-core the apples and place them in an oven-proof dish.

3. Fill the centre of each apple with the chopped walnuts, raisins and honey.

4. Bake the apples for 45 minutes or until they are tender.

Chocolate orange mousse

Serves 6

1 small orange
120 g (4 oz) 70% dark chocolate
6 large eggs
1 tbsp icing sugar/powdered sugar

1. Coarsely grate the zest of the orange and set it aside. Then squeeze its juice and also set it aside for the time being.

2. Break the chocolate into pieces and melt it in a bowl over a saucepan of boiling water.

3. Once the chocolate has melted and is smooth, take the bowl off the saucepan and let it cool for a couple of minutes.

4. Carefully separate the egg yolks from the whites and put them into separate bowls.

5. Beat the yolks into the melted chocolate.

6. Slowly pour the orange juice into the chocolate mixture, stirring constantly.

7. Whisk the egg whites until they become stiff.

8. Add the sugar into the egg whites and carefully fold it in with a metal spoon (this helps to retain the air bubbles as much as possible).

9. Carefully fold the beaten egg whites into the chocolate mixture.

10. Spoon the mixture into six ramekins.

11. Sprinkle the grated orange zest on top of the mousse.

12. Place the ramekins in the freezer for at least 3 hours.

Apple crumble

Serves 4-6

Filling

4-5 ripe sweet eating apples (Pink Lady or Gala are the best)

Crumble

60 g (2 oz) ½ stick unsalted cold butter + a little extra for greasing the baking dish

120 g (4 oz) ¾ cup wholemeal/whole wheat flour

120 g (4 oz) ¾ cup ground almonds/almond meal

2 tsp sesame seeds (optional)

2 + 1 tbsp caster sugar/fine granulated sugar

1 tsp ground cinnamon

1. Pre-heat the oven to 180C/350F/gas mark 4 and grease a 20 cm (8 inch) baking dish with a little butter.

2. Start by making the crumble: chop the butter into small cubes and put it into a mixing bowl.

3. Add the flour, almonds and sesame seeds, and rub the butter into the dry ingredients with your fingertips. The crumble should be the consistency of breadcrumbs – but don't worry if the mixture is a little lumpy.

4. Mix in 2 tablespoons of sugar. Place the crumble in a fridge while you prepare the apples.

5. Wash, core and chop the apples into tiny pieces (it's important to make them as tiny as you can so they will be soft when you take

the crumble out of the oven). I leave the apples unpeeled, but if you want to peel them, that's fine too.

6. Put the apples into the baking dish and spread the crumble over them.

7. Mix the cinnamon with the remaining spoonful of sugar and sprinkle the mixture over the top of the crumble. This will give the crumble a toasted appearance.

8. Bake the crumble for 15-20 minutes or until it has become golden brown.

Creamy custard

Serves 4

300 ml (10 fl oz) 1 ¼ cups whole milk

1 vanilla pod*

4 large egg yolks at room temperature

1 tsp honey

1 tsp grated nutmeg

1. Pour the milk into a saucepan.

2. Cut the vanilla pod in half with a sharp knife, scrape the seeds and add them as well as the pod into the saucepan.

3. Put the egg yolks into a bowl and whisk them until they become frothy.

4. Gently heat the milk on a low heat, stirring constantly so it doesn't burn. When it comes to the boil, slowly pour it in with the egg yolks, whisking constantly.

5. Pour the mixture back into the saucepan.

6. Gently heat the custard, stirring all the time. Shortly it will thicken slightly.

7. Take the saucepan off the heat promptly as too much heat will make the custard curdle. Stir in the honey.

8. Spoon the custard into 4 ramekins, sprinkle the nutmeg on top and place them in the fridge for a couple of hours – the custard will thicken when it cools.

* Substitution

If you can't get hold of vanilla pods, use pure vanilla extract or powder instead.

Note that if vanilla pods are rinsed and dried after every use, they can be used many times – although the strength of the flavor will lessen.

Cinnamon pears

Serves 6

6 pears

3 tbsp honey

3 tsp ground cinnamon

125 ml (4 fl oz) ½ cup water

1 star anise

60 g (2 oz) ½ cup chopped walnuts

Single cream/half-and-half or light cream for serving

1. Pre-heat the oven to 180C/350F/gas mark 4.

2. Peel the pears, cut them in half and core them.

3. Take an oven-proof dish and place the pears in it.

4. Drizzle the honey and sprinkle the cinnamon evenly over the them.

5. Pour the water around the pears and add the star anise into the water.

6. Bake the pears for 35 minutes, then take them out of the oven and sprinkle the chopped walnuts over them.

7. Return the dish back into the oven and bake for another 10 minutes.

8. Take the pears out of the oven and remove the star anise. Arrange the pears in serving dishes and wait for 10 minutes before serving them with some cream.

Baked goat's cheese figs

Serves 4

8 fresh figs
60 g (2 oz) soft goat's cheese

1. Pre-heat the oven to 200C/400F/gas mark 6.

2. Cut each fig into vertical quarters without cutting all the way through to the bottom.

3. Place a little goat's cheese in the middle of each fig.

4. Put the figs into an oven-proof dish and bake them for 20 minutes.

Apple and raisin bake

Serves 6

6 eating apples

6 tsp raisins

Juice of an orange

6 tbsp water

6 tsp sesame seeds

6 tbsp chopped almonds

1. Pre-heat the oven to 180C/350F/gas mark 4.

2. De-core and chop the apples into small pieces. I don't peel them, but if you want to peel yours, you can of course do so.

3. Put the apple pieces into an oven-proof dish and scatter the raisins over them.

4. Squeeze the juice of the orange over the apples and raisins, and also pour the water over them.

5. Place the dish in the oven and bake for 15-20 minutes.

6. Take the dish out of the oven and sprinkle the sesame seeds and almonds over the apples.

7. Return the dish to the oven and bake for another 10 minutes or until the apples are soft.

* Serving idea

If you like cream, you could serve this dessert with a few table-spoons of single cream/half-and-half or light cream.

Recipe index

Luscious Books is an
independent publishing house
specialising in wellbeing titles.

Find more cookbooks for special diets at

www.lusciousbooks.co.uk

8601448R00062

Printed in Germany
by Amazon Distribution
GmbH, Leipzig